Rules for (My) Life

The Beginner's Guide to Living a Life You Love

Jason Van Dyke

Cover Design: Jason Van Dyke
Editor: BVD Freelance Designs
Interior Design: BVD Freelance Designs
Publisher: BVD Freelance Designs
Author Photograph: BVD Freelance Designs

ISBN: 979-8-9990128-0-7 (paperback)
ISBN: 979-8-9990128-2-1 (eBook)
ISBN: 979-8-9990128-1-4 (audiobook)

Printed in the United States of America

To Duane and Christine,
for giving me a bedrock of faith.

To Mark and Matt,
for showing me your road maps.

To Zach and Ethan,
for sharpening my iron.

To Bree,
my love, my light,
for being my greatest support and best friend.

Contents

Introduction

Everyone lives by a set of rules, a way of making decisions.

Did you choose them for yourself, or are you doing what someone else has told you to do?

"Live a life by design, not by default."
                    -Shiv Khera

This is a book about the rules I use to guide my life.

When you picked it up, maybe you were thinking,

> *Yes, just what I need – more rules to live by and to observe.*

Or perhaps you simply want a little more structure to an otherwise chaotic existence. Maybe you're even here to pick my brain about my thoughts on certain topics.

Whatever your reason, I'm glad you're here. Welcome to this book.

I think you'll find this to be a little different from other self-help books.

My hope is not to preach at you or point out all the ways in which you're not doing enough or failing at life. There are enough critics in the world, so I don't want to add to those voices.

This is simply a conversation – well, maybe more of a monologue, *technically*, since I can't hear your response.

But all the same, my desire for this book is to bare my heart – to reveal how one person out of the billions on this planet has decided to live his life.

I've experienced and learned many things with the help of my parents, friends, mentors, teachers, professors, and other sages and guides.

Hopefully, you recognize that some of the greatest influences in your life can come from anywhere – from someone's passing comment to a thought-provoking classroom lecture. If you keep your ears open, you can gather wisdom, insight, and understanding from a multitude of sources – and hopefully be better off for it.

That's what this book is: nothing more than a collection of things I (try to) live by.

Maybe you find the idea of "rules to live by" to be restricting, but everyone has a set of rules they live by – filters through which they see the world and make decisions.[1]

Whether you like it or not, your life is already a result of the way you live. I haven't encountered many people who have an *intentional* plan to live by, but everyone has some kind of plan.

Think of it more as a "decision-making framework" that transforms my intentional decisions into automatic responses over time.

When faced with a decision in life, these ideas give me a clear direction of what I need to do to be the person I want to be. This list isn't about "Here is what I can and cannot do," but rather, "I've pre-decided how I want to show up in the world, and this plan aligns my actions with my intentions."

I just tend to think of them as rules, but you and I can disagree about semantics.[2]

I believe the question is not "Do I live by rules and principles?" but "*Whose* rules and principles do I live by?"

At a high level, these rules are composed of your values and beliefs, either purposefully decided upon for yourself or adopted from what others say.

---

[1] For more on this idea, I recommend checking out the chapter "How? A Rule of Life" in John Mark Comer's *Practicing the Way*.
[2] "Guiding principles" if that's more your jam.

Life rules (or principles) are handed to us through things like cultural messaging, parental values, and generational traditions.

Voices speak into our lives from every direction, some quite loudly and others more softly. These voices could come from our friends, peers, parents, boss, coworkers, teammates, an advertising firm, a TV commercial – the list goes on, and I think you get my point.

That's why I'm convinced everyone has a plan like this – because if you don't decide on one for yourself, society is eager to make it for you.

Once a rule is given to us, we either refine them through self-reflection, asking if they still serve us well, or we simply hold onto them for no other apparent reason than not taking the time to ask ourselves, "Do I still think this is valid? Is this the way I want to live?"

Let me come down from my soapbox and get back to what I was saying.

Some of my rules and sayings are things I repeat to myself daily, and others I only need to remind myself of once a month or on some kind of special occasion. These rules are unequally applicable across my life – some only work at certain times. But each one shapes my life in profound ways.

After living with these rules and sayings for this long, I don't think I could – or would want to – go back to life before them. With a clear process for how I make decisions in my work, my relationships, and for myself (my soul), I have found greater joy, peace, patience, sanity, and hope for the future.

Some philosophers say we (as people) are defined by the decisions we make. I think "defined by" might be a little strong, but our decisions certainly contribute to who we are. The same is true for me and my rules – some of them make me the person I am.

Speaking of which, this is a good time to introduce myself.

I'm a twenty-six-year-old graduate student pursuing a degree in marriage and family counseling after spending four years in the corporate world as a software developer. Confronted with my own shortcomings, I started exploring self-help and self-improvement over a decade ago, reading every book I could get my hands on.[3]

I have the privilege of sitting with people and walking beside them as they navigate their lives, discussing everything from day-to-day frustrations to life-changing challenges.

I don't always have answers, advice, or the right thing to say, but I promise to sit with people in the middle of their struggle.

But this book isn't so much about who I am.

This book is about *why* I am.

I invite you to sit down and read this book as though we're getting coffee together and I'm simply sharing my thoughts with you.

Furthermore, I invite you to wrestle and dialogue with what I'm saying. If there's a rule that clicks for you in the way I describe it, that's fantastic.

But if you need to take what I've written and tweak it to fit your life, I think that's even better. I don't claim to have answers to

---

[3] At the time, I had greater access to books than all the podcasts and YouTube videos we have in the self-help space today. We're in quite the resource paradise – what a time to be alive!

everyone's life – I simply have found what makes my own life better.

If you absolutely hate the rules I live by – you now have a better idea of what you *don't* want.

You and I live different lives, and you're faced with different decisions than I am. You will probably be best served by adopting a decision-making process that's different than mine.

This book is nothing more than a starting point for you to define *your* process. However, I think there's a strong possibility that these "rules as written"[4] will help you in similar ways to how they've helped me.

I encourage you to take them as they're written here, think about them, chew on them for a while, and then decide what works for you. Remember, it's about asking the question, "Would this serve me well? Is this the way I want to live?"

I ask that you bring an attitude of gentle skepticism with you as you read this book. I promise to be honest and "speak plainly"[5] with you, reader, if you promise to test what I'm saying against your own personal experience.

I also think it's important to note from the get-go that I'm a Christian. I will reference the Bible a few times because it influences how I make decisions.

Regardless of whether you subscribe to a faith tradition, identify as a spiritual person, or are wholly separated from a belief system, I've tried to provide you with a tangible place to start when it comes to creating your own decision-making process.

---

[4] Shout out to my Dungeon Masters in the audience.
[5] Foreshadowing.

While this book is written from my Christian perspective, I promise you do not need to be a Christian or even religious to gain insight or find a rule that applies to your life.

I don't expect you to agree with everything I say, but I expect you to consider how you've chosen the life you have and the ways in which you've allowed other people to shape your life for you.

Thank you in advance.

This book is divided into three sections.

The first section outlines rules that apply to my daily tasks and other work I need to do. When deciding what to do in the face of a task or chore, these are the things that help my life run a little smoother and help me crush my to-do list so that tasks never pile up.

The second section focuses on rules that influence my relationships and act as guiding principles for how I interact with others in my life. These rules increase love, decrease tension, and make it more pleasant to live with other people.[6]

The third section is the largest and probably the most helpful; this section explains the rules for my soul. When it comes to my sanity, my quality of life, or simply cherishing being alive, these rules tell me where to go and what to do.

If any of these rules resonate with you or inspire you to make some changes, I'm so happy to hear that. This is part of my road map, and if it helps you navigate your life as well, that's amazing.

---

[6] And probably make it more pleasant for other people to live with *me*.

However, if you don't adopt any of these for yourself, I won't take it personally. At the end of the day, it's your life; I want it to be one that *you* love, not a life I've prescribed for you.

Before we begin, I want to clarify one final time that the goal of this book is not to get more people to live the same way I do.

When I look at the lives of my friends, my peers, and the world in general, I see too many people "letting life happen" to them instead of deciding "this is the way I want to live." I'm convinced we have more agency than we give ourselves credit for. My desire is that more people take ownership of their life instead of accepting whatever falls into their lap.

This is the way I've taken ownership of my life. I hope it can help you get a clearer picture of what you want for your own life so that you can live a life you love.

I'm glad you're taking a step with me on this journey.

And now, with the ground rules laid...

I would like to share with you some rules for my life.

Rules for Work

I live by rules that make the mundane and difficult tasks easier to handle, which help me avoid unnecessary stress in my life.

The Two-Minute Rule

If a task takes two minutes or less to complete, do it now; don't put it off.

Alright, we're starting off with a quick-hitter. I heard this rule as part of a YouTube video by Gabe Bult[7] about some of his minimalist practices.

I come back to this rule nearly every day because there's always something small that I've been putting off for a day or two... or week or two... and it just needs to get *done*. Or it's something in the moment that I don't have the motivation to do, like taking out the trash.

> *I need to finally bring that box in my office down to the basement for storage. I need to put that important letter in my filing cabinet. I need to bring some dirty dishes to the sink rather than letting them sit on the coffee table. I need to grab a screwdriver and tighten that screw that's making the cabinet hinge wobbly.*

This is the rule I turn to when I'm confronted with a tiny chore that I could either handle immediately or push off until later.

In practice, this simple rule eliminates the little clutter and chaos around my house that, after a while, adds up to something that makes me lose my cool (not that I have much of that anyway, but... I want to keep as much as possible).

I'm sure you've experienced coming home after a long day at work, and the dishes have piled up in the sink, and there's stuff

---

[7] Bult, G. [Gabe Bult]. (2023, October 23). *10 minimalist rules that changed my life* [Video]. YouTube. https://youtu.be/PO_Vw_j1OZY?si=g-mjpmGTdIqP_Sqr

cluttering your bedroom, and you need to add that one item to the grocery list before you forget again, AND you need to clean up after your dog or small child, AND you have to send that email before tomorrow's meeting, AND – you just want to SCREAM.

That's the pain point for me. It doesn't take long for the little things to add up. When they add up, they tend to become overwhelming, turning into a far larger chore than if I had just done it immediately.

Pushing off the chore until later saves me some energy right now, but handling it now frees up my time later for something important. I consider it an investment in the quality of my life later.

I understand this rule feels like a "Just do it! Suck it up!" kind of rule where I force myself to do things I don't want to do. I don't like the idea of forcing myself to do work against my will, so something I've noticed that is important to mention is that you might need to consider what barrier you face in completing these "two-minute tasks." It might not be what you think.

As an example, taking out the trash doesn't usually take more than a few minutes, but I still feel resistance toward doing this chore. One day, I asked myself what part of this chore I enjoyed the least, and I was surprised to find that the difficulty for me wasn't in grabbing the bag, tying it up, or taking the full bag outside to the trash can – I felt the most drained when I had to take extra steps to walk to the cupboard where we keep our trash bags, grab a new one, and put it in the garbage can; it just felt tedious!

Once I recognized where the real obstacle was, I changed how I go about taking out the trash. Instead of first taking the full bag out of the garbage can, I now start by grabbing a new bag and bringing it with me over to the garbage can. This way, when I tie up the full bag and pull it out, I can set it aside and put in the new one without moving another step.

Now that I have a new routine for completing this chore, my lack of motivation to take out the trash has almost entirely disappeared. All it took was asking myself if there was a specific aspect of the chore that could be improved and then finding a better way to do it.

When I stick to this rule, I retain some peace and sanity, knowing that life is running smoothly, with the little things in their place.

With this rule, I'm confident that I'm being the best husband, friend, and coworker I can be: I don't let messes pile up around my home, which would drive my wife bananas; I don't forget to write down an important memo from my friend; I don't leave messes or simple tasks for others to handle.

Most importantly, I take care of myself by keeping my personal space (e.g., my home office, my car, my side of the bedroom) clean and organized; if I want to function at my best, I need tidy personal space.

With this rule, the little things stay little rather than growing into something frustrating.

And little things are always easier to take care of than big things.

Don't Forget to Remember

Don't forget what the other side of a difficult or tedious task feels like. Let that satisfaction motivate you to get the task done.

The last time I mentioned this rule to someone, they chuckled at me. I must admit, it *does* sound a little funny.

"Don't forget to remember" – at best, it's oxymoron-adjacent.

However, I think it's been one of the most profound rules in my life.

This one comes from Dr. John Delony, mental health expert and internet personality.[8] He described this as a helpful phrase for individuals with ADHD to hold onto to remember the tasks that are so easy to put off or to forget.

Allow me to set a scene:

One thing I love waking up to in the morning is a clean kitchen. I love the feeling of waking up in the morning and walking into the kitchen with the sun shining through the window and the sink empty of dishes. I can start making my coffee in peace, without the apprehension of adding another mug to the mountain of dishes in the sink.

As much as I love waking up to no dishes in the sink, I don't have the same affection for doing the dishes right before bed. I'd rather go straight to sleep. I'm tired, it's been a long day, and I've got things to do tomorrow that require me to get to bed. Right. Now.

---

[8] Delony, J. [The Dr. John Delony Show]. (2024, July 9). *Write this down... remember Monday...* [Video]. YouTube. https://youtube.com/shorts/CCHC8lZUh2U?si=jj-8dUztA42okDF_

And those are the moments that make the biggest difference. When I'm faced with the choice to call it a night or to knock out the dishes, I remind myself:

> *Don't forget to remember how good it feels to wake up to a clean kitchen. Don't forget to remember how much brighter the day starts when there aren't any dishes in the sink.*

Oftentimes, that thought is enough to motivate me to do the dishes before bed.

Realistically, by doing the dishes before bed, I don't spend *that much* extra time awake. It isn't a big deal when I think about it logically. But mentally, it's a hurdle to jump over, especially if I have genuinely had a tough day.

By allowing the post-chore satisfaction to be my motivation, I step up to the task from an affirmative position of "I'm doing this so that I can enjoy the benefits thereafter," instead of from a self-destructive place of "I need to do this or else I'm lazy/a loser/[insert your negative self-talk here]."

But doing chores before bed isn't the only area where this applies. I often remind myself:

> *Don't forget to remember how good it feels to be caught up on homework before playing video games.*

> *Don't forget to remember the sense of satisfaction when my priorities are in the right order.*

It even applies to things I want to avoid:

> *Don't forget to remember how crappy I feel when I eat a bunch of junk food immediately before bed. So don't do that.*

This rule helps me do hard things. Or more accurately, they're "hard" things because they require me to act like a responsible adult. However, they're the foundational things I need to take care of in order to live the life I want.

If I wake up to a pile of dishes in the sink, my day is noticeably duller and more tiring compared to when I didn't forget to remember.

When I allow homework or other things to intrude on date night with my wife, I start to feel anxious, guilty, and overwhelmed. Inversely, when I remember to plan around my priority of spending time with family, my life unfolds exactly the way I like it.

Similar to the previous rule, this one cuts down on clutter, both physically and mentally. This rule brings peace into my life and helps me relax at the end of the day because I know I'm taking care of the things that need to get done, which is one of the ways I try to care for myself and others.

For me, there are few feelings better than waking up after a good night's sleep, walking into the kitchen with the sunrise peeking through the kitchen window and the sink completely empty.

It all starts when I don't forget to remember.

Deep breath in

Deep breath out

>Oh yeah. It's going to be a good day.

And with that, I'm going to go do some dishes.

Rules for Relationships

I live by rules that reduce friction and ease tension in my relationships with other people, which lead to more life-giving relationships that feed my soul.

Memories, Not Materials

Don't hold onto items that are cluttering your life only because they're from someone you care about or from a trip you took.

I've been on a few trips to different states and countries so far, and there's usually a designated time during my trip when I think, "Alright. Time to find a souvenir. Should it be a T-shirt? A coffee mug? Something else?"

Consequently, over the years, I've ended up with dresser drawers and storage boxes full of t-shirts, mugs, and other trinkets from my trips that, if I'm honest, I don't use very often, and I only bought them to commemorate visiting a new location, as if I'll somehow forget the trip or lose the photos I took.

Similarly, I've received a few items that formerly belonged to family members who have since passed, or family members have given me gifts that I feel obligated to keep around because they're from family.

I can't get rid of gifts from *family*, right? What kind of heartless son/nephew/grandson would I be to do that?

I feel tension in those moments between trying to honor the ones who gave me the gift (or honor the person who has died) and knowing that I don't need/don't want/won't use the item.

I don't like the feeling of only keeping something around for the sake of being able to say, "Yes, I still have it. My conscience is clean, and I'm honoring the people who gave this to me or the person to whom this once belonged."

That tension is hard for me to navigate. I'm a people-pleaser to my core, and my inclination to help others and hope they're pleased with me is what motivates my decision to hold onto these items that I don't need/don't want/won't use.

But finally, I heard someone else going through this same dilemma, and what he said changed my life.

Dr. John Delony (of earlier-in-this-book fame) described receiving his late grandfather's suit upon his passing. He said for the longest time, the suit simply sat in his closet because 1) it wasn't the right size for him to wear, so he couldn't use it, and 2) the thought of giving it away made him feel guilty because he thought he'd be letting down his grandfather.

I'm going to paraphrase, but the way he reconciled this tension was by reminding himself of the truth: "My grandfather isn't in this suit. He's in my heart. And I love him. I miss him. But he's right here, in my heart. The memory of him is still with me, and whether I have this suit of his or not doesn't change that."

Delony decided to give away his grandfather's suit.

And that story has set the course for how I handle similar situations in my life.

For example, I feel guilty throwing away old birthday cards that people sent me, even from ten-plus years ago.

They went through the effort of getting me a card and wishing me a happy birthday; I should keep this card in honor of that effort.

So I remind myself:

*My grandmother/aunt/parent/friend isn't in this card.
I appreciate the birthday wishes they gave me, and I know
they still support me. I'm going to choose to throw away this
card so that I have less clutter and fewer belongings in my
house, which brings me peace; in the meantime, I'm holding
onto their love for me in my heart.*

The same rule applies to trinkets, articles of clothing, or anything else I've received from someone I love, or purchased for myself on a trip that I inevitably don't use.

When the item has reached the end of its usefulness to me, I choose to put a period at the end of that sentence.

*Thank you for giving me this. Your support means the world to
me. I love you, and I'm letting this go now.*

Get Curious

Keep an open mind and give people the benefit of the doubt. You never know when your assumptions might be wrong.

Curiosity is typically something we associate with children, nosy friends, and felines (often to the feline's detriment).

As I've grown older – moving from my college years to my young professional years, and now to my graduate student, counselor-in-training years – I'm finally starting to realize what a gift curiosity is, especially when it comes to how I relate with other people.

A question I've begun to ask myself when getting to know someone is, "Do I know *everything* there is to know about this person?"

The reason I find this question motivating is summed up in an article by Dr. Thomas F. Fogarty, entitled *On Emptiness and Closeness*.[9] He says, "When you know somebody, the relationship is ready for burial. If you know somebody, you lose interest in them and become more self-centered or look elsewhere for interest and enthusiasm."

If I claim to know everything there is to know about someone else, then I close myself off to new ways our relationship can grow. In this case, Dr. Fogarty is right – "The relationship is ready for burial" – and that's not usually a thought I like to have about my relationships with others.

So I ask myself, "Do I know everything about them – *literally* everything, from how they react to their favorite sports team losing to their thoughts on a recent social issue in the news?"

---

[9] Fogarty, T. F. (1973). *On emptiness and closeness – Part I. Compendium I, The best of the family* (p. 78). The Center for Family Learning.

The answer to this question is an obvious, "No, I don't."

And that means there's more to discover about this individual whose company I'm in.

More people than just jetsetters and beer commercial guys have interesting lives. Everyone lives an interesting life with interesting stories to tell – if I'm willing to take the time to get to know them.

But not only is this useful in the early stages of a relationship; it's also useful in understanding my closest relationships more deeply.

I think it's reasonable for me to say that curiosity is the opposite of judgment. And when someone close to me, like my wife, for example, does something that bothers me, frustrates me, or anything like that, which reaction would I rather have? Curiosity or judgment?

I want to get curious, which means I choose to keep an open mind and move forward with curiosity.

Do I know *exactly* why she did the thing that bothered me? I can make guesses and assumptions, and maybe my guesses get more accurate the longer we're married...

But no, I probably can't know *exactly* why she did what she did unless I ask her.

If I react with judgment – with a harsh tone and by saying something like, "That thing you just did doesn't make any sense. I don't know why you did that." – how would that make her feel?

First, a harsh tone will immediately put her on the defensive, and she'll feel forced to justify her actions. We're already off to a poor start if we want to have a productive conversation.

Second, look closely at the statement I just made: *"I don't know why you did that."* What does that statement reveal? I've just admitted that there's something going on here that I don't know. And that something might be important.

By reacting with judgment from the start, I tell her, "You're unintelligent, you're incapable, and you can't accomplish this task."

My wife is a smart cookie. She has a lot of good reasons for the things she does. She's certainly not unintelligent or incapable. So what am I missing?

Oh yeah, it's probably that *something* I allude to when I say, "I don't know *why* you would do that."

I.e., her good reason for doing the thing she did in the way she did it.

Most of the time, if something like this happens – she does something that makes no sense to me – I just let it go and choose to believe the best in her, assuming that she must have a good reason for it, whether I care to know the reason or not.

But other times, when the thing she does really bothers me, and I want to understand what was going through her mind when she did it, I choose to approach the situation with curiosity.

For example, my wife works from home a few days out of the week, which means she typically has the chance to take fifteen minutes to do some chores when she's on a work break. Sometimes I ask if she could do the dishes while I'm at work because she happens to have more time to do the dishes than I do that day. Sometimes, on those days, I come home to dishes still in the sink.

Here's the fork in the road: she either blatantly ignored my request, choosing to be lazy and not do the dishes like I asked, even though she knows how much it means to me to have a clean sink; or...

"Hey, honey. It must have been busy at work. How was your day?"

I want to get curious about what might have kept her from doing the dishes. Sure, there are times when she chooses to put off doing the dishes because she doesn't feel like it. I understand that; I've been there too. But sometimes she genuinely is swamped all day with meetings, aligning calendars, and completing all the things her team relies on her for.

We might eventually come back to a conversation about how she didn't do the dishes like I asked her to, but that conversation comes second to asking her about her day so that I can understand what happened. If this was a busy day for her, I have no right to demand she do the dishes when her work is a higher priority.

Sometimes she did have time and didn't feel like doing the dishes. No big deal: either I can do them myself, or we can have the conversation of how doing the dishes would have really helped me out with the other things I need to do at home.

Do you see the difference here?

One of these responses accuses, "You didn't do what I asked you to do! You must not care about me!"

The other asks, "What happened today that overloaded you? What did you need a break from? How can I help you and love you best?"

It's subtle, but it makes a world of difference.

Judgment causes tension.

Tension strains relationships.

Curiosity eases the tension.

So whether it's getting to know someone new, or assuming the best about the people I love, I choose to let curiosity be my guide.

Otherwise, I might end up with a relationship that's "ready for burial."

Invitations, Not Accusations

Invite others into your world by starting with "I"; share your perspective and experience before critiquing theirs.

Hopefully you're already familiar with the concept of 'I' statements, but in case you aren't, here's a short example:

Instead of telling someone, "You did this and hurt me," you instead say, "I felt hurt when you did this."

See? 'I' statements simply express the situation from your point of view, which is helpful when it comes to discussing emotional or sensitive topics with someone else.

Statements like these are so powerful because they invite someone else into your experience in a way that allows them to know you and maybe even help you solve a problem.

'I' statements communicate that the things you're sharing are your personal perspective, and not necessarily an objective problem with the other person. I find that people are less likely to get defensive about something expressed from my perspective.

Let me use a more complex, hypothetical example to illustrate my point.

Let's say one of my friends is in a dating relationship – we'll call her Shannon – and, based on what she has shared with me about the relationship, I think her boyfriend, Chad, isn't treating her the way she deserves to be treated. We'll say in this scenario, I don't want them to break up, but I want her to address the problems with her boyfriend so they can have a happier relationship.

One way to approach this conversation would be to say, "Chad doesn't treat you right. You deserve better."

This approach blames Chad for being the problem, and I force Shannon to either take my side against her boyfriend or to defend Chad, which could drive a wedge between us.

Alternatively, if I choose to invite her into my world, it might look something more like this:

> "I'm concerned that you deserve to be treated better in your relationship. Based on what you've told me, I get the sense that Chad doesn't treat you very well. I want to support you, but I know I don't have all the details. What am I missing?"

When I choose to invite Shannon into my experience, I acknowledge reality, which is that, based on the limited information I know about their relationship, I'm convinced that Chad isn't treating her the way I believe she should be treated.

It's entirely possible that Chad is a terrible human being. I might coincidentally be correct that he doesn't give her the respect or dignity she deserves.

But I'm not the one in the relationship, and I don't know her boyfriend like she does.

Instead of coming out swinging by saying, "Chad is a problem" – which, again, may or may not be true – I choose to share my perspective: "I'm not convinced this is good for you, but I recognize that I might be missing something. Will you help me understand?"

In this made-up example with Shannon and Chad, I'm not accusing Chad of being a terrible person; I'm inviting Shannon to help me see the bigger picture of her relationship. I'm asking her to help me deal with the pain that I feel for her because I think she's being mistreated.

In its essence, this rule is for those situations when I can't take care of a problem on my own and need the other person's help, like in the example with Shannon and Chad. Based on my perception of the situation, it's true that I feel hurt for Shannon. But it's *her* relationship, so the only way to address my pain is to talk to her about it. I might not have the whole picture, so I'm going to need her help to fill in the gaps.

Here's another example of how this rule applies to one of my own relationships: let's say I'm in a tough situation with a friend where we keep fighting and can't seem to agree on anything. If we want to fix our relationship, we probably need to sit down and talk about it.

That conversation could go in one of two ways:

> "You're wrong about this. You don't understand that. You're the problem here and need to change."

Or...

> "I don't want our friendship to fall apart because of this argument. I'm willing to explain my side of it and own everything I did wrong. Do you want to work together to make this thing awesome again?"

Invitations, not accusations.

It's too easy to blame others for a relationship problem in front of me. Fortunately, if I invite them in by sharing my experience and asking for their help, I know we can solve the problem together.

I Only Speak When I Can Be Heard

I don't share my opinions or ideas with people who can't hear me or who won't listen to me.

Have you ever had a mental conversation with someone (more of an argument, really) to point out what they're doing wrong?

In your mind, you explain why they're foolish for doing what they did, and they admit that if only they had listened to you, things would have been better off; they recognize the error of their ways and promise to change for the better.

Anyone else experience that? Just me?

I find myself in this position all the time, especially when it comes to driving. When I'm behind the wheel, I find myself frequently saying,

> "Why are you going so *slow*? Don't you know the speed limit is 55, not 52?"

> "Oh, I'm sorry your turn signal is broken, otherwise I know you would have used it."

But the problem with this is that no one can hear me because they're in a different vehicle. Besides, even if I could get the other driver's attention by doing something like flashing my headlights, there's no possible way I could give them my gentle advice on how they can improve their driving in a way they'd genuinely listen to and take to heart.

Situations like this remind me that there are simply times when people don't want to hear what I have to say.

Whether it's advice, offering correction, or expressing my opinion, the reality is that my words won't always be received with open arms and open ears.[10]

I can't do anything to control other people or how they react. The only thing I can control is how I respond to people when they behave a certain way – like cutting me off on the freeway, for instance.

Maybe you've had a situation like this, where you've given good advice to a friend – like, *really* good advice – but your friend decided to continue in the direction they were heading before you shared your genius idea with them.

Frustrating, right?

I don't want to drive myself crazy by trying to share my thoughts with those who don't want to hear them.

Aside from the physical reality of not being able to converse with people in other cars on the road, even if I could somehow sit down with these other drivers and explain how to properly use their turn signals, would that go well for me?

How likely are they to genuinely listen, take my advice, and make changes in their behavior?

I think we both know the answer to that one.

So I choose to save my breath and let it go.

If they aren't going to listen, then why do I need to make it my problem? There's no reason to be concerned unless I choose to

---

[10] Something about horses and water, or pigs and jewelry...

dwell on it. At that point, I'm only choosing to make myself miserable.

At the end of the day, it's their life. They must live with the consequences of their actions, not me. Why do I need to get riled up over something that won't affect me?

The same rule applies to my interactions with extended family, in-laws, friends, coworkers, etc. If they're not willing to listen to what I have to say or have made it clear that they're not open to my advice, what do I gain by choosing to make it my problem?

In return for dwelling on their actions, I'm likely to have anxious thoughts, some bursts of anger, and I'll enjoy my day that much less.

Yeah, sign me up.[11]

This rule gives me more peace in my relationships because I only try to control the controllables, and I choose to let go of everything else. I don't need to waste my mental energy solving other people's problems when other people don't see them as problems at all and don't need me to solve them.

My life has enough challenges caused by my *own* behavior, let alone trying to correct someone else's behavior when they won't even listen.

Before I share my opinions and advice with others, I wait until they ask. If the situation is dire enough, I bring up my concern as someone who loves them and wants what's best for them by "getting curious" and relying on "invitations, not accusations."

---

[11] I hope you can hear my eyes rolling.

By combining these rules, I release the things that I have no control over, share my experience of what it's like to be in a relationship with the other person, and keep an open mind to what they're going through.

Like I said in the previous chapter, these rules are all about choosing to live in reality.

I choose to avoid having imaginary arguments with people in my head – even though I always win.

I choose to let other people live their own lives, including all the good and bad that comes with it.

And hey, if you ask for my help because your actions have led you into some tough places, I'll be there to walk with you out of it.

And maybe I'll tell you "I told you so" when it's all over.

Rules for My Soul

I live by rules that bring peace to my body and mind, which help me build a non-anxious, unhurried life that I love.

Be A Gatekeeper

Monitor what goes in – it determines what comes out.

Jesus of Nazareth said, "...it is not what goes into the mouth that defiles a person, but what comes out of the mouth; this defiles a person."[12]

There's an immense amount of context surrounding this statement that I'll choose to omit for the sake of brevity, but the gist of what Jesus is saying is, "Pay attention to what comes from your heart."

What comes from my heart (my words, my thoughts, my reactions, etc.) is the result of the entertainment and content I consume, the music I listen to, and the things I allow myself to dwell on.

When I listen to mainstream pop music, I feel myself becoming less joyful and more apathetic. When I watch YouTube videos that criticize other people, I'm more judgmental toward others. And when I mentally fixate on hypothetical scenarios of what could go wrong today, I'm more anxious and on edge, actively looking for the next threat.

My mood shifts for the worse, I snap at people I love, and I'm far less patient when small inconveniences come up.

Once I recognized this and started thinking about how I wanted to change it, I became much more decisive about what I gave my attention to. I set some ground rules for what kind of content I consume.

For example, I spend a lot of time during the day exerting mental

---

[12] Matthew 15:10b-11.

energy on things like work and school. When I have a chance to relax, I want to mindlessly consume a YouTube video or play video games. However, if I "turn my brain off" to give it a break, then I allow myself to be affected by anything that is put in front of it.

Like I already said, sometimes the content I consume shouldn't be allowed into my brain without some intentional filtering.

I don't want to be less joyful. I don't want to be more judgmental. I don't want to feel anxious.

So I choose to do things differently than before.

I love listening to music. As good music should, the music I listen to influences how I feel and even what I think about. Recently, I've traded the pop music for lo-fi or synthwave music to relax. This chill instrumental music gives me something to listen to in the background when I'm doing chores or driving to school, but it doesn't have any of the negative side effects that other genres of music with lyrics can have on me.

If I try to relax by watching a YouTube video, I stay away from anything critical or deeply thought-provoking because my brain needs a break from deep thinking. I can't have a mental break *and* monitor the videos I'm watching at the same time.

I used to play video games to relax, but I've recently considered letting that go as well. A friend of mine challenged me that, "Maybe those video games and your other forms of 'rest' are actually cluttering your brain more than helping it relax." I couldn't help but feel there was some truth to his statement.

With all that in mind, I've started resorting to pure silence as a valuable form of relaxation. Some days while I drive to work, I leave the radio, Spotify, and podcasts turned off. Sometimes I do the dishes or take out the trash without headphones on. Sometimes my brain needs space to process what's happening in the moment or what has happened earlier in my day.

My brain can't process the things I experience if I'm constantly bombarding it with new distractions and noise from YouTube, music, or other content.

If my form of rest is giving my brain a break from the thought-provoking things I've engaged with all day, then my brain truly needs space to breathe and not think about something new.

This rule takes intentionality and discipline. Our world is so noisy with its notifications, content creators, and endless advertisements. If I don't carefully watch what I let into my life, my life starts to look noisier and more chaotic, just like the rest of the world.

But I'm better off when I'm in control of what I'm thinking about, whether it's the peace and calm of chill music, or the occasional informative podcast.

It all depends on what I choose to let in.

Facts Are Your Friends

I choose to live in reality rather than dwell on things that haven't happened or simply aren't true.

I choose to live in reality. And the reality is that my emotions don't always tell me the truth.[13]

So if I can't find truth in my emotions or my feelings, that means I need to find the truth somewhere else – the facts.

My boss gave me feedback at work recently – the constructive kind in which she said, "I've noticed this pattern, and I think you could work on this."

If you'll allow me to be transparent, I walked away from that meeting feeling far more unsettled than I should have. My emotions were at an eight when I know, logically, they should have been no more than a three or four.

I started thinking more about the situation by asking myself, "Why am I *this* bothered by what she said?"

I replayed her words in my head: "*I've noticed a pattern...*"

I realized I was convinced that if she had noticed a pattern of my behavior over time, then she must have been annoyed with me this whole time. My internal voice started up:

> "My boss is annoyed at me. She doesn't like me. She practically hates me, I bet."

---

[13] Delony, J. [The Dr. John Delony Show]. (2023, November 6). *Why you can't trust your feelings | The 6 daily choices* [Video]. YouTube. https://youtu.be/PFqnFcAmV_0?si=pZacMlKWwWow-dh4

Wait a minute...

Where was all this coming from? Why is this the story that starts playing in my head when someone shares feedback with me?

More importantly: *What evidence did I have that my boss was annoyed at me?*

She gave me valuable feedback. She wasn't trying to hurt me; she was trying to help me improve as a young professional. She didn't have malicious intent by telling me how I could do better. And the reason she shared the feedback only after noticing a pattern over time is because she doesn't see the value in trying to fix what could possibly be a one-time fluke.

The idea that my boss was annoyed at me came from the people-pleaser inside me that wants everyone to like me.

I wrote down and listed the facts:

1) The conversation started because I asked her if she had any feedback for me.

2) She wants me to be the best young professional I can be.

3) We have a good working relationship, and I trust her to tell me the truth.

So when I started hearing the internal story that she's annoyed at me – when I started feeling anxious and afraid that everything was coming down around me – I turned to a practice that in cognitive-behavioral therapy terms is called a "Thought Record."[14]

By taking the time to ask myself, "Why am I *this* bothered?" I provided room for my thoughts and emotions to tell me why I was convinced my boss was annoyed with me.

Here's what the process of using a Thought Record looks like:

I sat down in my office at work, took out my Thought Journal, and put the story in my head onto paper:

> *My boss is annoyed with me. I've been annoying her for the past few months with my behavior. She probably hates me.*

And once it was in front of me, I took a breath, read it back to myself, and wrote immediately underneath it,

> *Is that true?*

Is the story I'm telling myself true? Who says? What proof do I have to support this narrative in my head?

My emotions were sounding the alarms, but I think more often than not, emotions are meant to protect us rather than give us factual evidence. I knew this story wasn't true.

My emotions were just trying to keep me safe because when people don't like me, then they might hurt me. And I don't want to get hurt.

So what was true?

---

[14] And the little notebook in which I keep these records is called my "Thought Journal." I know it sounds kind of crazy, but I carry it everywhere I go, and it's a lifesaver.

I wrote it out:

> *My boss appreciates my hard work. She told me she likes working with me because I'm thoughtful and intentional about what I do. I know she wants the best for me, and she would never tell me something just to hurt or insult me.*

And then I continued thinking and writing about the situation as a whole:

> *This feedback is just a normal "down" in the "ups and downs" of any kind of relationship. I think most relationships start off strong, and then usually there's some kind of "down," or challenge, that the two people in the relationship face. If they put in the work to make things right, the relationship comes out on the other side of the challenge even stronger than before.*

Fact: This is normal.

Fact: My boss doesn't hate me.

Fact: If I put in the work to change my behavior and embrace the feedback she gave me, then we'll be better for it.

I'll be better for it.

But it all started by recognizing that my emotions were doing their job perfectly; they just weren't helping me reach the best conclusion.

In this situation between my boss and me, my emotions were telling me to run away, hide, fight, and do other unproductive things. If I chose to listen to them, then I would have been safe. If I had listened to the emotions instead of confronting the voice in my head, I would be more guarded in my relationship with my boss moving forward.

But then she wouldn't know me. There would be a whole part of myself I'd be leaving at home when I go to work. My work would be different, the interactions I have with others would be different, and it's possible that the work I need to do just wouldn't be done effectively.

But at least I'd be safe, right?

It sounds selfish when I lay it out like this. And I think it's selfish in this scenario. But that's what my emotions are for – they try to keep me safe and don't always take others into consideration.

That doesn't mean I can ignore them; they keep me safe, *and* they're meant to be felt.

Emotions don't tell me the truth, but I still need to acknowledge them. I can't shove them aside or stuff them down, otherwise I can't live the full human experience.

In the 2012 movie, *Thanks for Sharing*, Tim Robbins' character summarizes this perfectly:

"Feelings are like children. You don't want them driving the car, but you don't want to stuff them in the trunk either."[15]

In the situation with my boss, my emotions were trying to get my attention. They were trying to get in the driver's seat in order to protect me.

---

[15] Blumberg, S. (Director). (2012). *Thanks for sharing* [Film]. Olympus Pictures; Class 5 Films.

Thank you for trying to keep me safe, emotions. But I'm OK. I'm in the driver's seat. And the fact is that my boss is just trying to help me.

I can recognize my emotions *and* allow myself to feel them without allowing them to take over.

But in order to do that, I need to stick to the truth.

My emotions keep me safe, but facts are my friends.

The Only Way Forward is Through

Nothing in my life gets better if I sit on the sidelines waiting for things to change. The only way to get past the challenge I'm facing is to tackle it head-on.

I face challenges (broadly speaking) quite often, including sitting down to do homework.

I don't usually want to do homework.

And I don't want to do other hard things, like file my taxes, or work out, or have tough conversations with my friends.

It'd be easier to bury my head in the sand, ignore the problem altogether, and indulge in escapism by playing video games or watching YouTube.

Maybe you've tried this strategy before, too.

But, without fail, when I'm tired of playing games and watching videos, my problem is still there.

Nothing has changed, except for the fact that I now have less time to work on whatever I need to do.

Cue the stress.

Why do I do this to myself? Why do I choose to run away from my problems instead of choosing to deal with them?

Maybe you've asked yourself the same questions.

I believe the answer is quite simple: It's easier to run away and ignore a problem than to face it head-on.

Temporary relief (e.g. video games, YouTube, TikTok, social media) is just that – *temporary*.

At the end of my escapism, I'm still left with a problem/challenge/issue that needs to be addressed.

I don't know about you, but I don't have Robin Williams' Genie in my life that magically fixes all my problems for me.

It's my life, and if I don't handle it, no one else will.

I've run away from my problems enough to know that all I get from running is wasted time. So instead of wasting even more time, I've decided to start taking control through action.

The only way this gets better is if I do something about it.

No one's going to do this homework for me, so I better start working.

That tough conversation isn't going to start itself, so I better make the first move.

Insert your scenario here.

It's not going to change on its own.

Inaction improves nothing.

Okay, fine. I'll admit that inaction can handle *some* problems, but it usually only creates new ones:

Yeah, I could choose *not* to do my homework... and get a poor grade in the class.

Yeah, I could choose *not* to have that conversation with my friend... and then maybe not have a friend at all.

Yeah, I could choose *not* to file my taxes... and owe the government a bunch of money or end up in jail.

So even if someone else takes charge, or I just hide until the problem turns into something else, this allows someone else to control my life.

I want my life to happen on my terms rather than allowing life to happen to me.

If I want the best possible life, then I need to make a choice and do something. I'm not going to sit idly by and allow my life to be dictated by other people or by other circumstances.[16]

The only way for me to move forward, beyond the hard thing, is to run straight into the middle of it.

I'm not waiting for the door to a great life to open for me. I'm going to break it down.

The only way forward is through.

---

[16] You could consider this the central thesis of the book.

Live With Margin

I refuse to live an anxious life, worried about my time, money, and other resources. I'm going to give myself room to breathe so that I can navigate challenges with peace and dignity.

Have you ever had a flat tire? Or maybe an unexpected medical bill? Or any other type of sudden emergency or urgent issue? The breath catches in your chest as you recognize that you don't have the time or money to handle the problem.

Do you remember the stress of the situation? You may have experienced uncertainty, wondering what you would do to return to normal life. Maybe you said, "I don't know how I'm going to pay for this," or you asked the question, "What do I do now?"

That feeling has been very familiar to me when I live my life at the edge of my limits – financially, relationally, or temporally.[17]

Life without margin feels like there's a constant buzz going on inside of me; it's the pit in your stomach when there's too much month left at the end of your paycheck; it's the hustle and hurry of sprinting to your airport gate because you slept in just a little too long and were late arriving at the airport.

Life without margin feels like you can't catch your breath and there's

noroomtobreathe.

It's agitation. It's anxiety. It's worry and uncertainty.

---

[17] That'd be "with my time."

It's lightning in your body and a nuclear reactor in your chest.

And everyone around you can feel it.

You're a ball of energy, moving from one thing to the next.

Never sitting still.

Never taking a moment to relax.

Never...

Inhale

Exhale

...breathing deeply.

I've been there, when my back is against the wall, and I'm *barely* holding it all together, knowing that if one more thing goes sideways, it will all come crashing down.

> "I need these bald tires to last another month because I just don't have the money to replace them."

> "I hope people won't mind that I'm running late to my meeting."

> "This is the third time I've messed up this report. I hope my boss looks past it just *one* more time."

Do any of these situations sound familiar?

You're stretched far too thin, and everything must be perfect for it to work, because if it isn't *just right*...

...the plates I'm spinning will topple and shatter on the ground.

Is that the way you want to live? Constantly running, running, running, trying to fit in every possible thing?

Our society says we can do it all if we just balance it all perfectly.

I'm tired of my life being a circus act. I'm not a world-class juggler; I'm just a normal human being.

I'm tired of rearranging balances on credit cards because I just need this one card to have enough credit to cover my rent.

I'm tired of trying to fit in four one-on-one coffee dates with friends because "I'm a terrible friend if I don't make time for everyone."

I'm tired of trying to force a single day to be the place for my yoga class, a perfect date with my spouse, finishing my quarterly report, and making sure my dog has all the love and affection it requires to think I'm Pet Parent™ of the Year.[18]

> *There's got to be more to life than hurrying, hustling, running, and balancing. Right?*
>
> *What about resting, relaxing, and laughing?*
>
> *That's the life I want.*

I want to have the breathing room to give my full attention to the things I say "yes" to. I want my "yes" to actually mean "I'm here for this" instead of "You have my *divided* attention for the next half-hour, but I'll be thinking about my next meeting the whole time."

---

[18] I don't know if this trademark exists, but it just feels like something I'd see on a tabloid cover in the checkout line.

I want to look back on every piece of my life and be able to say I was intentional; to be able to say, "I *chose* that, and it made my life better."

I was reminded of what this looks like during my most recent visit to the Denver International Airport. My wife and I were walking to our gate to catch our flight, and as we passed by the restaurants, I looked at the people inside, sitting and enjoying their meals.

And I thought, "I know we don't have time for this today, but wouldn't it be amazing to be at the airport and have an extra $60 in our budget and an extra two hours to spend sitting down and enjoying a calm and delicious meal?"

Imagine having the financial and temporal margin to sit down at an airport restaurant, let your shoulders drop, breathe a sigh of gratitude, and be able to say, "I'm going to enjoy this meal because I know I have the money to pay for this, and I'm early for my flight."

Maybe margin looks like working hard for one week at work so that when Saturday comes, you can go to your favorite coffee or ice cream shop, sit down with no agenda, order whatever you want on the menu, and know that you get to enjoy that time and food, your mind free of worries about to-do lists or money.

No hurry.

No hustle.

No stress.

Just peace.

I've said a lot this chapter without getting to what this rule looks like. That's because, for me, the ultimate outcome of this rule is a feeling more than a behavior.

So I wanted to paint a picture of what your life could feel like if you stopped trying to balance it all, do it all, and have it all.

A picture of what my life looks like now that I have

room   to   breathe.

What this rule means for me is that my wife and I choose to have financial margin by creating a budget and sticking to it.[19] We have an emergency fund and a buffer in our checking account to avoid any overdraft fees.

It means I create margin in my calendar by leaving an extra five minutes for myself to get a drink of water or use the restroom before my next meeting so that I'm not in a rush or possibly late.

It means I only schedule what I know needs to be done today because I can't possibly do it all at once.

It also means I intentionally say "no" to things I love and want.

I've come to recognize if my "yes" is going to mean anything, then I must be willing to say "no" too.

No, I'm sorry. I can't get coffee with three people in a row today because I need time to spend with my wife, and buying three coffees probably won't do my wallet or caffeine tolerance any favors.

---

[19] We don't do this perfectly, but we're practicing.

No, I'm sorry. I can't go to that concert tonight because this paper is due tomorrow, and I don't want to be stressed out trying to pull it together at the last minute.

No, I'm sorry. I can't buy another video game, go out to eat, or get another piece of décor for my home because I need to save some money for those new tires on my car.

At work, there's a sign hung up that illustrates this quite well. It says, "Remember: You can do anything, but you can't do everything."

What would your life look like if you had the extra margin that you've always craved? If you didn't have to run from one commitment to the next? If, thanks to a budget, you knew for a fact that you could afford to buy milk and eggs, or fill up your car with gas, because you were intentional about the things you spent your money on?

What would it look like?

What would that *feel* like?

I'm willing to bet it'd start to feel like you can breathe again.

That's how it felt for me.

Live Slowly

I refuse to be hurried no matter how busy I am.

The world moves at such a rapid pace – and I don't mean the evolution of technology, medicine, or anything like that.

Mobile order pickup, side hustles, "I've got that grindset," and other similar ideas and services pervade our modern Western culture.

Instant messaging, instant gratification, and, heck, even instant noodles – "Instant" is the dominant format for how we receive information, entertainment, and nourishment.

When I look at the world, I see this prevalence of immediacy resulting in a rushed and hurried culture. A tired culture. And I'll argue that all the hustling and bustling is part of what's turning us into an anxious culture as well.

We were never meant to live instant lives.

But before you dismiss me as "hating the fast lane," I need to make an important distinction – I'm all for being busy, being productive, and getting things done; but I hate being hurried.

Yeah, that's right. Busy ≠ hurry.

John Ortberg, a Christian pastor, author, and speaker, describes the difference in technical terms: "Being busy is mostly an outward condition; it's a condition of my body. It's having many things to do... Being hurried is a condition of my soul."[20]

Just to offer a more tangible picture of this, Jordan Raynor, another popular author, says,

> I'm busy if I've got a lot of errands to run on a Saturday; I know I'm hurried if I get pissed off about choosing the wrong lane at the grocery store because I couldn't sacrifice the two minutes that I lost in picking the wrong lane.[21]

There's a distinct difference between what's on my calendar and what's in my soul. If I'm not careful, a full calendar or to-do list inevitably leads to a hurried soul. Maybe you've been there, too.

When I'm stretched thin in my responsibilities and obligations – when I've said "yes" approximately a bajillion-too-many times and don't have time to give my full attention to the things that truly matter – then I start to feel anxious and irritable. I get easily frustrated, and I tend to snap at the people around me. Especially if things aren't going *just right*.

I resonate with what Jordan said, that if I get angry because of an unexpected two-minute delay, then I know something needs to change.

The symptoms of a hurried soul include more than just anxiety, frustration, and anger – being hurried means I can never be fully present with the tasks and people in front of me.

---

[20] Global Leadership Network. (2013, August 14). *John Ortberg - Busyness* [Video]. YouTube. https://youtu.be/UY--SZUyIw8?si=XzPsbb6yiYCCzzjC
[21] Weber, A. [Adam Weber]. (2025, May 7). *Busy vs. Hurried with Jordan Raynor* [Video]. YouTube. https://youtu.be/Qm-ZQH0PV8k?si=yCgPVHh1dV-5O8UT

When I'm hurried, I'm always preoccupied with the next thing on my to-do list – that next project, assignment, or meeting to go to.

When I'm hurried, I end up robbing my professors and bosses of my best work and the people around me of the best version of myself.

When I'm hurried, I can only give a fraction of my attention to what I'm doing; and when I can't give my full attention to anything or anyone, every area of my life begins to suffer.

To avoid these situations, I need the following:

- Intentionality with my schedule
- Patience and humility
- New behaviors

When it comes to my schedule, this is where "living with margin" comes in. I choose to intentionally add margin between things like meetings, work time, and spending time with my friends and family so that I never need to rush from one thing to the next.

A helpful rule of thumb from Jordan is to add 50% to your estimate of how long you think a task will take – especially if the task is new to you or involves traveling to a new place.[22]

I also need to practice patience and humility if I want to avoid being hurried. This means I try to see the bigger picture when things don't go as planned (e.g. "The extra two minutes in the checkout lane won't ruin my day. I can still reach my destination on time"). If I'm late because of poor planning or something that's out of my control, then I apologize to whomever I kept waiting and ask for forgiveness.

---

[22] See note 21 for reference.

My new behaviors involve purposeful choices to slow down my body: I choose to walk across campus at a *stroll* rather than at a brisk pace.[23] I choose to take the stairs one at a time as often as possible. I force myself to move my body slower because when my body is hurried, my soul is hurried.

A quick caveat about this: If I've done a poor job of "living with margin," and I'm running late, I do try to move a little faster to be courteous to the person waiting for me.[24]

I also want to highlight the difference between being hurried and moving quickly – being hurried is a lifestyle of agitation and chaotic energy; moving quickly is a momentary action in a time of need.

In the event of an emergency or crisis, please move quickly if the situation requires it (while not making things worse). Arrive at the scene in record time, stop the bleeding, or go see your loved one as soon as you can. If the situation is dire, move quickly.

Being hurried refers to a way of living and moving through life – rushing from one thing to the next without taking time to give yourself or others the rest and attention you or they need.

To clarify: this rule is *not* about clearing your calendar and doing nothing with your life; you can be busy without being hurried.

For example, a previous boss of mine frequently spent the majority of his days in meetings. For any meeting he scheduled, he made sure it started five minutes after the hour and ended five minutes before the hour so that he had time to use the restroom, check his email, or have a quick conversation with a coworker if necessary.

---

[23] Assuming the weather outside is nice and not colder than the Arctic tundra like it tends to be here in the Midwest.

[24] Again, this is where humility and an apology come in, but I try to avoid keeping others waiting as much as I can.

This is something I admired about him because, despite all the meetings filling his calendar, he was never frantic or rushed, just excited about the work he was able to do.

I apply this rule in both broad strokes, like when I'm setting up my schedule for the week, and in moment-by-moment decisions, like when I walk downstairs to the basement – one-at-a-time it is!

This rule keeps me from getting sucked into the anxious and hurried rat race of everyone around me.

It means I live at a slower pace than the rest of the world.

It means I take time for things that truly matter and bring me joy.

It means I see the present as the most precious gift I have rather than speeding through it to get to the next thing on my calendar.

Living life slowly means I can be in the presence of someone else and say, "Whatever's next on my calendar comes second to being here with you."

Fair warning: I need to be up-front and tell you this was hard for me at first. The world doesn't often reward slowness, and there are plenty of voices that tell us to go faster. Pretty soon, a hurried life becomes our default, and we grow accustomed to being preoccupied with the next thing to do.

Time to confront a hard truth: maybe you're making the intentional choice to *stay busy*. To remain hurried. To always be preoccupied...

...because of what might come up if you allow yourself to slow down.

Let me tell you – being excessively busy and hurried is an effective drug when we need to escape from difficult feelings, difficult tasks, or difficult relationships. Being constantly preoccupied with that next item on the to-do list is a sure-fire way to keep emotions at bay when we're not ready to deal with them.

But if no one has told you already, let me be the first: constantly running away from something is a fast-track to burnout – physically, emotionally, and relationally. Running away works, but it won't work forever. You're only human, and you will reach your limits.

If this is you (and I've been there, too), I sincerely encourage you to sit down with a professional in your area and let them know what's going on – to tell someone what you're running from and why.

The people around you want you to be present, and you can't give them your full attention if you always have the next thing on your mind. Please slow down, both for them and for yourself.

If you keep yourself busy in an attempt to run away from something or someone – including running away from yourself – then you're probably going to hate slowing down. You're going to feel antsy, restless, and uncomfortable.

Ian Simkins said, "If busyness is your drug, rest will feel like stress."[25]

I already mentioned the first side of hurry – that it robs me of being present and focused with people, with tasks, and with the various aspects of my life.

---

[25] Simkins, I. [@iansimkins]. (2023, December 14). *I definitely say things like this as someone who has a long way to go.* [Tweet]. X. https://x.com/iansimkins/status/1735326427711472066

But the other side is the opposite – it *gives* me something. Hurry rewards me with a reprieve from things I don't want to confront.

That's a coin I don't want in my pocket, so I choose to set it down instead of carrying it with me.

I choose to "live slowly" and "live with margin" for a "so that." I live at a different pace and live with breathing room *so that* I can experience peace; *so that* I can be fully present with the people and activities that truly matter; *so that* I can enjoy life at my own pace, not at the breakneck speed dictated by everyone around me.

So that I can breathe, drop my shoulders, and relax.

So that I can enjoy the fruits of my labor.

By choosing to live slowly, I'm rewarded with intentional time with my family and friends, a deep sense of satisfaction with the life I'm building, stability and calm in the face of uncertainty, and genuinely liking the person I see in the mirror.

Living slowly is my way of taking back my life from the world around me. I hear so many voices speaking into my life, and all of them seem to say, "Do more, go faster, push harder."

I choose to listen to the voice from within that says, "You're doing enough, and you're doing a good job. Take your foot off the gas pedal. Enjoy the life that's right in front of you."

Look at Your Life

Progressing requires reckoning with reality.

Is it just me, or have the concepts of "mindfulness" and "journaling" really come into vogue in the past few years?

While I tend to roll my eyes at the mention of yet another "mindfulness technique," I have certainly come to appreciate the benefit of paying attention to my life – the things I do during the day, the things that happen to me, the conversations I have, and the people I spend time with.

I also like to process the things I go through – "debriefing my day," so to speak, so that I can recognize and acknowledge what happened.

I do this in a variety of ways, from talking aloud to myself on my commute to and from work, to typing in a journal Word document saved on a flash drive, to writing in my physical journal I bring along with me everywhere I go. My journaling process looks pretty similar to the Thought Record concept I shared earlier.

I usually begin processing by recounting the facts:

> "Today, I got coffee with my friend, James. He told me about some difficulty he's having at work, and I told him about what's new in my marriage. He's a single guy, so he asked me a marriage question, and I tried to give him my best answer."

Then I move into my evaluation:

> "Looking back, I realize I should have phrased my answer differently. I should have mentioned this or that, and I think

it would have made more sense to share my thoughts on this other thing, too."

Finally, I calibrate the way I *want* to think about this interaction:

"Oh well. I can't change it now. I'll just try to say it better the next time someone asks a similar question. I'm honored he saw me as someone that could provide him with the insight he was looking for, and I hope he still got some value out of it, even if it wasn't 'perfect' (whatever *that* means in this context)."

Hopefully you caught the simple formula: "What happened? What do I think? What would I do differently next time?"

It's a simple, but powerful, formula for walking myself through my day and unpacking the things that took place.

By processing my day, I give myself the chance to look at what happened and consider what I could do differently to get the life I want. If I want to grow as a person, I may need to make changes to my language or behavior.

And the truth is that I can't change what I don't acknowledge.

"I want to handle this differently" must be preceded by, "This is what happened."

Over time, I start to see more of what I write in the "do differently" category move into the "what happened" category.

When I mention the idea of journaling to others, I hear the response, "I don't have time for that; life's too short."

Having lived both sides of this equation, I argue, "Life's also too short to waste time on a life you don't love."

This rule is about taking time to recognize what needs to change in order to build the life I want.

You might refer to this as "journaling," "processing," "evaluating," or "manifesting" – call it whatever you want – but no matter how you think of it, taking steps in the direction you want requires giving some thought to the direction you're currently heading in, for better or for worse.

Similar to "live slowly," this rule results in a lifestyle more than a specific way of making decisions in-the-moment. However, it's this rule that helps me evaluate what kind of life my decisions are getting me.

As I stated in the introduction, I'm confident you have a plan that leads you to make all the daily choices that comprise your life.

The question is: *What are your current choices getting you?*

And perhaps the bigger, scarier question is: *Are they getting you what you want?*

I encourage everyone to take time to reflect on these questions. You ought to know what kind of life you're living, and you *really* ought to know if it's the kind of life you want. Because if it isn't, then you might want to start changing it sooner rather than later.

That's the good news: I can change the life I have.

Oftentimes (and especially in adulthood), we create the lives we find ourselves in, choice by choice. This means if we don't like it, then we also can choose something different, something awesome, something aligned with what we truly want.

For me, this evaluation of my life – this "reckoning with reality" – is comprised of two questions: "How did I get here?" and "What do I want to do now?"

"How did I get here?" means exploring my actions, the stories I tell myself, and my past – not with judgment, but with curiosity.

"Why did I respond that way? Why did I say that?"

"Who told me I'm not good enough? Who told me I'm unlovable? Who told me this story I'm believing right now?"

The answers to these questions come from reflection on your lived experiences thus far – and there's a good chance that some of these questions may lead you into your childhood experiences.

That's a scary thought for many people.

Unfortunately, "the only way forward is through."

There's no way to know who you are – or more importantly, *why* you are – until you've faced your own life and examined the things that have made you the person you are today.

I have yet to find an easier way to do this. Trust me, I'm all about efficiency and finding a simpler way to get things done, so if something easier existed, I'd tell you. But the truth is that if I want to get to know the person in the mirror, I'm going to have to learn about and explore the things he's gone through.

I can't blot out parts of my past that I wish didn't exist. Those things happened. No one can change that. All I can change is what I do next.

Fortunately, that's the other part of journaling – answering the question, "What do I want to do now?"

This is the part where I get excited and start to dream a little bit. After exploring how I arrived at the situation I'm in, I can begin to decide, "What kind of life do I want to live now?"

Here are a few sample questions to get you started:

"How do I want my home to feel when I walk in the door? Is there going to be peace? Laughter? Joy? Will I finally be able to drop my shoulders and relax?"

"What kind of relationship do I want? Are we going to be passionately in love? Are we going to have a hard time keeping our hands off each other? Are we going to be able to tell each other the truth? Can we support each other in the hardest times?"

"What impact do I want to have on the world? What difference am I going to make in someone's life?"

And the final, vital question:

"What must be true for all of this to become reality?"

I hope you're starting to see what answering this question has the potential to become.

You can use this to begin dreaming about the big things, but I think it's especially important to apply this to the day-to-day things, too:

"How do I want to respond when my friend tells me hard things like they did today?"

"What kind of employee do I want to be when my boss is acting like a jerk?"

"When my young kids are bouncing off the walls, how am I going to respond? Would I rather reinforce or replace the patterns my parents showed me?"

"When my spouse raises their voice at me, do I *actually* want to yell in return? Or do I want to be a calm presence that brings peace to my marriage?"

Do you see what we're doing here? Questions like this are about examining our situations and trying to insert just a little bit of breathing room – all you're looking for is one extra millisecond – between what's going on and what we do.

I want to be a person who *responds* instead of *reacts*.

I want to be a person who thinks before he speaks.

I want to be a calm presence for those around me.

I want to be a person who fills a room with laughter instead of sucking life out of it.

I want to be a person who brings peace to my relationships.

I simply want to be the best version of myself.

I'm willing to bet you want the same.

So how did you get where you are today? And what are you going to do now?

What kind of life do you want to live?

The changes you want to see won't just happen on their own. Getting to where you want to go requires intentionally looking into the mirror.

You're going to have to get to know yourself – your likes and dislikes, the ways you respond in certain situations, the ways you celebrate or shut down when people say or do specific things. You need to know who you are, why you are, and what you want.

Once you know where you are, then you can chart the course to where you want to go.

Borrow A Road Map

Get help from those who have gone before.

As I write this chapter, I'm 26 years and 185 days old. I know it might be hard to believe, but this is my first time being 26 years and 185 days old.

Okay, maybe it's not so hard to believe.

The point is that I'm totally new to this. With nearly everything going on in my life, I've never done any of it before.

I've never been this many years and days old; I've never lived today before; I've never been married before; I've never gone to graduate school; I've never written a book.

But there are people who have.

The human experience is unique to everyone, but the good thing is that no matter what I go through, there's likely to be at least *one* person who has gone through similar things. Maybe not exactly, but similar.

In navigation terms, there's likely to be someone who has charted that course, someone who's drawn that map.

Fine, I'll admit: some adventures in life are better when you wing it and just "go with the flow."

But when the stakes are high, and there's a chance someone could get seriously hurt, it helps to have a map from someone who has traveled to the place you want to go.

Life is hard. I think life is hard enough as it is even when you *do* know what direction you're heading in. How much harder is it when you don't know what direction to take?

King Solomon, one of ancient Israel's early kings, was lauded as one of the wisest men who ever lived. He wrote a bunch of his wisdom down in what would later become the book of the Bible called Proverbs.

I don't know about you, but if the wisest guy in the history of humanity wrote stuff down, I want to hear what he has to say:

"Getting wisdom is the wisest thing you can do! And whatever else you do, develop good judgment."[26]

What? The wisest guy ever tells us to get wisdom? Not a fat retirement account? Not fancy cars or watches? Not a six-figure job so that we can have comfortable lives?

He said, "...*whatever else you do*, develop good judgment." As in, "above all else, no matter what, if there's anything worth doing in life, it's getting wisdom and sound judgment."

He also says a lot more about how wisdom is more valuable than silver or gold (and crypto, I might add).[27, 28]

He says if you're wise, you're likely to live longer,[29] will live a more peaceful life,[30] and that you won't fall into the traps of others.[31]

Alright, I hope I've made my point: seek wisdom.

---

[26] Proverbs 4:7, NLT.
[27] Proverbs 3:14, 16:16.
[28] Come at me, Crypto Bros.
[29] Proverbs 9:11.
[30] Proverbs 1:33.
[31] Proverbs 2:12-15.

A quick refresher on wisdom: Oxford defines wisdom as "Capacity of judging rightly in matters relating to life and conduct; soundness of judgement in the choice of means and ends."[32]

If I were to paraphrase, I'd say wisdom is possessing good judgment that is informed by your experience.

It's important to note that wisdom and knowledge are not the same thing. As Miles Kington, the British journalist, says, "Knowledge is knowing a tomato is a fruit; wisdom is not putting it in a fruit salad."[33]

Knowledge and wisdom work together to help you navigate life's challenges. I usually find myself needing more of one, the other, or both as I approach these challenges.

Back to what I was saying at the start of this chapter: I'm currently navigating stages of life I've never been in before – married, a graduate student, an author – and so the best thing I can do (according to King Solomon) is to seek the wisdom of others who have already navigated these things. I should find out what they say so that I can do these things in the best possible manner.

That's why I like reading books on marriage, asking other graduate students about their experiences in our program, and looking up articles on how to write a self-help book for the first time.

I tend to find a bunch of stuff I didn't know before, things that will help me do my best in these areas of my life.

---

[32] Oxford University Press. (n.d.). Wisdom, n. In Oxford English dictionary. Retrieved May 19, 2025, from https://doi.org/10.1093/OED/3627755117

[33] Kington, M. (2003, March 28). *Knowledge is knowing a tomato is a fruit; wisdom is not putting it in a fruit salad*. The Independent.

A decade ago, I learned the importance and the value of having a mentor. When I was 16, my mom told me I was going to start meeting with an older gentleman in our church. His name is Mark.

Over the following two years, before I graduated high school, Mark and I developed one of the closest relationships I've had in my life.

He was far beyond me in terms of life – married, adult kids, grandkids, looking ahead toward retirement, all that stuff.

Because of his life experience, he had many wise things to tell me concerning the problems I was facing in high school. Had he not shared his wisdom with me, I'd probably have floundered far worse in my time in high school, and later college, because I had no clue what I was doing.

What he shared gave me an idea of what could come next – some of the things I should look out for, and also the things that I could look forward to.

It's like being on a long journey by yourself with limited resources and no map. You're just following the path and taking things as they come, with all of the path's surprises, bruises, and pitfalls.

Finally, you cross paths with someone who's holding a map that details the next part of the journey.

Wouldn't you want to look at their map? Don't you want to know what comes next? Wouldn't it be valuable to have something that would make the journey a little easier?

I felt this way shortly after my wife and I got married. Having never been married before, all the books I had read on marriage up to that point had given me some ideas about how to be married, but I was still lost and confused as to how to be a good husband. I felt like it was chaotic and like I was failing at every turn.

I found myself frequently saying, "I thought I'd be better at this. I thought I had the tools to do this."

This feeling continued until I realized that, in every other season of life since I was 16, I had had a mentor who could show me the path ahead, point out the things I needed to pay attention to, and warn me of the dangers I should avoid.

But I didn't have a mentor in the early months of our marriage. I was getting beaten up by all the new things we were experiencing. Yes, we were in it together, but I knew there had to be a better way than winging it.

I began asking around for a mentor, someone who could show me their road map for the early stages of marriage.

I was led to my current mentor, Matt.[34]

We decided to meet every other week, and as our meetings continued, I noticed that life was beginning to feel less chaotic.

I was finally starting to anticipate some of the challenges my wife and I might face. I began actively taking steps to navigate them with as little pain as possible or to avoid them entirely.

I found someone with a road map, and I stopped feeling lost.

Whenever I'm faced with a new situation or season of life, I seek help from someone who has done it before.

Whatever season of life you're in, someone has been there.

---

[34] I guess all the best Mentors have names that start with 'M.'

It might be someone you know personally, or maybe you'll need to find someone in a different part of the country or in the world.

Fortunately, this is where books, social media, YouTube, and online articles really shine. We have such easy access to the road maps of others to the point where we really have no excuse to not look at one.

Maybe you've been a trailblazer so far. Your "go with the flow" attitude brings excitement to your life. Maybe it's worked for you in the past, and maybe it will keep working for a while.

Or maybe you've been hoping for a road map for a long time. You're lost in the weeds, desperate for a way out.

Either way, there's someone who can help you navigate the road ahead. You don't have to be lost.

You just have to keep your eyes open for that fellow traveler with the map.

Do the Next Right Thing

I'm going to focus on taking the next step instead of trying to figure out all the steps. I'm going to do whatever is the single right thing to do next.

This rule is simple, yet effective, making it quick and easy to implement (like the two-minute rule).

Dallas Willard, a modern philosopher who had much to say on the topic of Christian spiritual formation, was once asked, "How does a person become a saint?"

Willard's response, as recounted by his mentee, Gary Moon, was simply, "By doing the next right thing."[35]

I think this is a powerful statement for spiritual formation. Some groups of Christians have made following Jesus a complex jungle gym, but this simplifies everything.

This statement also has immense power as a general life principle. I find it incredibly liberating and calming at the same time.

Let's say you "look at your life," and you identify some things you want to change. This rule helps answer the question, "What do I do now?"

I'm going to do the next right thing.

That's all I can do, to be honest.

---

[35] Moon, G. W. (2009). *Apprenticeship with Jesus: Learning to live like the Master.* Baker Publishing Group.

Sure, I can take time to plan out the next ten things I want to do or write a laundry list of changes I want to make, like a list of New Year's resolutions that inevitably come to a screeching halt by February.[36]

That's part of my problem: I am ambitious and excited about how to make the changes I've always wanted to make. I start daydreaming about how amazing my life is going to be once it all gets done.

But a week later, nothing has changed, and I've lost that spark that motivated me in the first place.

Believe me, I felt the same way about this book. I started getting excited about the idea of writing a book, about sharing the news with people around me, and what it would mean for my life now that I'm an "author."

But I've been on this rollercoaster enough times to know that unless I focus and actually take action, this book would end up like all my other ambitious plans – the plans, dreams, and wishes in my head that never make it into the real world.

So what did I do?

I did the next right thing – or in my case, I did the next *write* thing.[37]

I started small – making notes, clarifying my vision and intent, and just getting something typed.

I wasn't concerned with making it perfect – I started with a rough draft and refined it after that. And I didn't need to worry about

---

[36] January Jason is one of my favorite people. February Jason frustrates me.
[37] I've been told puns are the lowest form of humor, but I'm not above using them.

editing, publishing, or marketing.[38]

I knew nothing would get done if I didn't start somewhere. So I focused on the step that was right in front of me – creating a Word document to begin the writing process.

Then I started outlining what the chapters would be, what the book would be about, what resources I would need to write it all out.

I only did the next right thing for my situation. And then I did the *next* right thing. And the *next* right thing after that.

That's what this rule is about. It brings all the chaos under control, and it focuses my energy into one productive step at a time.

It's easy to get overwhelmed when thinking about accomplishing life plans, especially big dreams like going to college, starting a business or career, and raising a family.

There's a lot out there that is out of your control or that's simply out of reach for now. If you want to start a business, you need a product to market before you form an LLC. You need to establish an exercise plan before you start to lose weight or get in shape, even if that's as small a step as "I will walk for 20 minutes per day."

One thing at a time. Which one thing?

The next right thing.

Some of you might ask, "How do I know what the next right thing is?"

---

[38] Although, my brain *did* jump to those things before I reined it back in.

That's why I put this rule near the end of this book. If you've been following along – "looking at your life" and "borrowing a road map" – then I'm confident you'll have an idea of where to go next.

Worst case scenario, you could ask a generative AI tool like ChatGPT, Microsoft Copilot, or Google Gemini for next steps based on what you want to do. I don't always trust the idea of AI worming its way into every aspect of our lives, but I must admit these tools are fantastic for condensing vast amounts of data into bite-sized tidbits.

If you've taken some time to "look at your life" and have narrowed down what you want to do, explain your vision to one of these tools and ask what next steps you can take.

You could also look for resources online and "borrow a road map" from the Reddit users or YouTubers doing the things you want to do.

That's the other beautiful thing about this rule – if you don't know where to go yet, the only thing you need is the next step. You don't need to iron out the whole plan, just what comes next.

And from there, it becomes about working up the courage to take the next step.

And I've got one more rule for that.

Walk With God

My life will mean nothing if I'm only living for myself. I need to look to something bigger than me and trust that I don't carry everything on my shoulders.

"Enoch walked with God..."[39]

Once again, I'm a Christian, so the idea that I would "follow the rules of my faith" probably seems obvious.

Yes, this is part of what this rule does: remind me to make decisions that align with my beliefs.

However, if we take a step back, this rule is about more than the Christian faith, and even bigger than faith in general – it's a reminder that there's something bigger than I am and that my life isn't all about me.

You don't have to be religious, pious, or even spiritual for this rule to apply to your life.

"Walking with God" just sounds really cool to me.

Do you have something in your life bigger than you that influences your decisions? Maybe this is your family, a volunteer organization, or some other good cause you believe in.

Without something bigger to live for than yourself, you may wind up living a life of hedonism.

Hedonism is the philosophy that teaches life's greatest goal

---

[39] Genesis 5:34a.

involves the pursuit of pleasure and the avoidance of pain.

This typically sounds like, "I do what makes me feel good," or "I pursue whatever makes me happy."

From what I've seen and the stories I've heard, living a hedonistic life leads to really high highs, but also very low lows. Many people living this way are left wondering why they feel so empty.

Have you heard of rich people saying, "I have every possession I could want, and yet, I still can't find happiness"?

That's hedonism.

Or should I say, that's life without a bigger purpose.

I had a conversation last year with a follower of Santa Muerte, a personification of death associated with healing, protection, and safe passage from this life to the afterlife.

While I'm sure this guy and I would disagree about a number of things, we agreed that living life for ourselves is pointless.

In his words, "If you've got nothing bigger than yourself to live for, then you're just a [expletive] shell of a human being."

I agree. Minus the expletive.

Imagine that – a Christian and a follower of Santa Muerte finding common ground.

In his book, *Building a Non-Anxious Life*, Dr. John Delony describes "choosing belief" as one of the six daily choices we need to make to live what he calls a "non-anxious life":

Choosing belief comes in two parts: letting go of control and anchoring into the Source. Letting go of control is fairly self-explanatory. You must release the idea that you own your loved ones, should dominate the lives of your kids, employees, clients, or friends, or need to have input regarding all the world's affairs. At the same time, you have to believe you are anchored into something bigger than yourself. Something that operates within you, through you, and beyond you. Something that was before you and that will be after you.[40]

Delony emphasizes that we need both – we need to relinquish control, *and* we need to believe there's something more.

This is a challenge for me. I'll be honest, I like being in control. But I know that the universe doesn't revolve around me, so I need to give up control sometimes. And that becomes easier for me to do when I believe something bigger than me exists and *is* in control.

If your "something bigger" is your family, this might mean you remind yourself that how your spouse acts or how your kids turn out is not your fault – they have free will and get to make their own choices.

If it's your job or a volunteer opportunity, then maybe this means bringing your best to each task but exhaling in the fact that a tiny mistake won't bring the entire organization down.[41]

For me, this means I trust that God is bigger than I am and that he has far more control over my life's circumstances than I do.

Furthermore, I believe that God never changes, which means I

---

[40] Delony, J. (2023). *Building a non-anxious life* (p. 228). Ramsey Press.
[41] I know there *are* some jobs where this is the case. If you're in one of those jobs, please be very careful in what you do. For the rest of us, one mistake is usually not this catastrophic.

always have a solid "Source" to "anchor into." This is not the case with a lifestyle of hedonism – if every decision I made was an effort to pursue pleasure or avoid pain, I'd change my mind every day (more like every *hour*) about what matters most to me.

When I choose to live for myself, I inevitably end up letting myself down through foolish decisions and pursuing things that aren't in my best interest.

But when I surrender control and choose to "walk with God," my life begins to flourish.

In the movie *Rudy*, our football hero is discouraged about his prospects of playing for Notre Dame, so he seeks advice from Father Cavanaugh. When Rudy speculates that he hasn't "prayed enough," and asks the priest for help, Father Cavanaugh replies, "Son, in thirty-five years of religious studies, I've come up with only two hard, incontrovertible facts; there is a God, and, I'm not him."[42]

There is a God, and I'm not him.

That's the simple truth this rule reminds me of on a daily basis.

There is something – Someone – bigger than me.

I need to live for more than myself. Also, I'm not the one in control, as much as I'd like to think and act like I am.

By following this rule, I've been amazed at how freeing it truly is to admit I'm not in control. I trust that there's a God who cares about me, that he has good plans for me, and that I don't need to carry

---

[42] Pizzo, A. (Producer), & Anspaugh, D. (Director). (1993). *Rudy* [Film]. TriStar Pictures.

the weight of the world on my shoulders.[43]

Choosing to walk with God doesn't make life easy, but it definitely makes the inevitable hardships more bearable. It means I remind myself that I'm not alone, and that I don't need to worry about trying to be perfect all the time.

Spoiler alert: I'll never be perfect. None of us can be, no matter how hard we try. But that doesn't mean the pressure to perform goes away.

Does it feel like everything is up to you? That if you let things slip, then your life, or the lives of those around you, will be ruined?

Having been there myself, I want to invite you to let that go. It's not all on your shoulders. I used to think everything was up to me— that one wrong move could unravel everything. But the world has been spinning long before I arrived, and it will keep turning long after I'm gone.

Note to self: I'm not big enough, strong enough, or powerful enough to ruin God's plan for my life. He's much bigger than I am.

The same goes for your family, career, or other group activities – chances are you probably don't have the power to "ruin everything" on your own.

When I finally chose to let go of that crushing belief, something shifted. I could breathe. I could bring my best, knowing that even if I failed, it wouldn't destroy everything.

My shoulders don't hold the world. I trust there's something greater at work. And that frees me to finally live.

---

[43] That'd be a heck of a chiropractor visit, huh?

Daily Sayings

Little sayings I frequently repeat to remind me of important truths I want to embrace. These aren't rules, but they still help me be the person I want to be.

"Notes for next time."

In the spirit of having a growth mindset and embracing opportunities to improve, whenever I make a mistake or do something incorrectly, I say, "Notes for next time," to remind myself that I'll have another chance at this, and that my mistake isn't the end of things. It means, "I'll make a mental note of how to do better for next time." It's a way of removing shame from my mistakes and not beating myself up over what I did or didn't do.

When I "look at my life" and consider the things I tell my friends or the situations where I could have said or done something different, this phrase keeps me grounded in recognizing that I can't change what has already happened. Nothing I say now will change the past. The only thing I can do now is keep moving forward and try to do differently in the future.

"Slow is smooth; smooth is fast."

This is an operating principle of the United States Navy
SEALs. The way I understand it, in order to get good at doing
something (i.e. doing something quickly), you first need
to slow down and learn how to do it smoothly. It places
emphasis on deliberate, accurate actions to achieve
efficient, effective results.

My life's circumstances don't involve the intense situations
SEALs find themselves in, where being able to do something
smoothly (and therefore, quickly) is a matter of life and
death, but it reminds me to slow down and do things
correctly the first time.

If you've ever missed the garbage can when trying to throw
away a piece of trash from across the room, and then had
to go pick it up, you know it would likely have been faster to
simply walk the piece of trash to the garbage can in the first
place.

Ultimately, this saying boils down to a reminder that doing
something right is more valuable than doing it fast, especially
if my ragged attempt to do it fast will cost me more time in
the end.

"Voluntas Dei est" – ("It is God's will")

This Latin phrase is significant to me in ways that combine the sentiment of "Notes for next time" and "Walk with God."

This phrase reminds me that, if I believe God is in control, then I choose to believe things happen for a reason, even if I don't see it.

I've learned to let go of things and relinquish control by reminding myself, "The circumstances played out the way God wanted them to. If he wanted something else, then something else would have happened."

A quick caveat: I recognize that as you look at the history of world religions, a lot of harm has been done in the name of "doing God's will."

This saying is not that.

I'm simply trying to remind myself to stop overthinking everything because I don't need to be perfect.

When I'm beating myself up over what I did or didn't say, did or didn't do, then I tell myself, "Voluntas Dei est." I don't need to see the whole picture to trust that God will use whatever I said or did for good. I said what I said for a reason, and likewise, I didn't say what I didn't say for a reason.

It's not on me to control everything. So I remind myself to say, "It was the will of God," and then I give myself grace to move on because I can't control it all.

"Deo volente" – ("God willing")

This is another reminder that I'm not in control.[44]

"The heart of man plans his way, but the Lord establishes his steps."[45]

I can make all the plans I want, but if God is in control, then there's no way I can do the things I want to do without them being part of his will.

This is true for the big things, like moving or switching jobs, and the little things, like going to the grocery store or visiting a friend.

The Apostle Paul ends his letter to the Roman church with a similar statement, by asking for the Romans' prayers, "so that by God's will I may come to you with joy and be refreshed in your company."[46]

I'll go to school – God willing.

I'll watch a movie with my wife tonight – God willing.

I'll wake up in the morning to work out – God willing.

This book will be a hit when it comes out – God willing.

I trust that everything is in God's hands, so the only way I make plans these days is "God willing."

---

[44] I didn't realize until now how many of those I needed, but apparently, I have a lot of them.
[45] Proverbs 16:9.
[46] Romans 15:32.

"Lo barato siempre sale caro." –
("The cheap stuff always costs a lot.")

I'm not rich. I don't usually have the money to buy nice things. Sometimes, I have to settle for the more affordable versions of items. And sometimes, I'm a cheapskate, and I cut corners to save money by buying cheap stuff.

But those cheaper things tend to be of lower quality, and then they break, which means I have to go buy a new thing.

Buying two things is usually more expensive than just buying one thing from the start.

This phrase is vital in the moments when I try to cut corners, not so much when I genuinely can't afford to buy a nice thing.

It reminds me that, yes, I'm spending more money in the moment to purchase a higher quality item, but short-term loss means long-term gain if it saves me from buying another one in the future.

I find this is true about shoes, jeans, sunglasses, electronics, and a number of other small items. Cheap stuff actually can end up costing you more in the long run.

"Speak plainly."

No one benefits by beating around the bush.

Whether I'm telling a friend about updates in my life, or I need to give someone bad news – clear is kind, and I shouldn't tip-toe around or avoid what's truly going on.

The kindest thing I can do for someone is to be straightforward in what I tell them.

Rather than beat around the bush by saying something like, "Yeah, I'm alright. I mean, things are OK. Could be better, I guess," I choose to jump right into it by saying, "I'm not doing well. Life really sucks."

In a conversation years ago with my best friend, I was hiding behind fancy words, and he interrupted me by saying, "Speak plainly."

What he was telling me was, "Tell me what's truly going on. Don't mask it. Don't hide it. Tell me how you are."

My friends can only help me when I'm direct and honest with them.

Similarly, when it comes to delivering hard truths, people deserve to be told up-front.

This doesn't mean I go out of my way to be rude or heartless in what I have to say, but sugarcoating something that's difficult to hear doesn't help anyone, and it certainly doesn't help me express what's on my mind.

Who do I help by attempting to curate what needs to be said?

No one, except maybe my own self-image.

I'm not going to ask people to read my mind.

I'm not going to make a situation worse by "not getting on with it."

I choose to honor other people with the truth.

"Awareness is the first step."

When I'm confronted with changes that need to be made, I need to focus on one thing at a time. Understanding what the "next right thing" is has to start somewhere.

It might be a change that I need to make in myself, or a change that I'm helping a friend see in their own life. Either way, I try to offer encouragement by saying this phrase.

I don't want there to be any shame in myself or in others when we admit there's a problem or that we've made a mistake.

In order to address a problem, you have to be willing to admit there's a problem that needs to be addressed.

And we also don't need to go off the deep end trying to fix everything overnight. Awareness is just the *first* step. The rest of the hard work comes later and will be addressed with time.

I first choose to be proud of having the awareness to see a problem. And then I put in the work to change it after that.

"Doing nothing means doing everything."

I'm often too busy to get anything done. I used to say "yes" to too many things, and I used to be stretched too thin; I said all this earlier in the book, and maybe you can relate.

Do you know what happens when you try to do too many things at once?

Nothing gets done.

Brian Tome, founding pastor of Crossroads Church in Cincinnati, Ohio, cut right to my heart:

"The point is, distracted and fragmented lives rarely make a difference."[47]

I want to make a difference in this world. And I've seen too many instances in my own life where I agree to take on too much, and then the important things never get done.

If you want to reach the end of your life without getting anything accomplished, then stay busy with things that don't matter.

I had to face this hard truth in the past couple of months. I had to cut out a lot of things from my life, like watching YouTube, playing video games, and other obligations I had agreed to but that didn't contribute to my vision for my life.

Trust me, some of these things are really good things, and you can invest your time in good things all day long.

---

[47] Tome, B. (2018). *The five marks of a man: Finding your path to courageous manhood* (p. 46). Baker Publishing Group.

But if you don't have time to invest in your life's purpose, then does it matter? Are you going to reach the end of your life knowing you lived the life you want?

Or will you look back on your life wishing you had said "no" to more of the distractions that crowded out your purpose?

In the aftermath of some hard conversations about stepping back from some of my obligations, I felt like I was doing absolutely nothing – which was true, compared to how busy I've kept myself for most of my life.

Back to what Ian Simkins said: busyness is a great drug. When I mentioned ways of numbing my feelings and not feeling them, keeping yourself busy is one of the best methods of numbing in America.

That's not a good thing, by the way.

So I realized that by not doing things that don't matter, I finally have time to do everything that truly matters. It's almost paradoxical.

This phrase reminds me to evaluate and be intentional about what I give my time to. It reminds me that if I want time to do things that matter – spending time with my wife, writing a book, editing my podcast – then I need to actually build in time to do those things.

And I won't have time to do those things if I'm constantly giving it away to activities that don't pour into my life's purpose.

Sometimes you must choose to do nothing in order to get anything done.

"Guilt over resentment."

Dr. Gabor Maté says, "If the choice is between resentment and guilt, choose guilt every time."[48]

The spirit of this idea is that if you have to make a choice between establishing boundaries for your own well-being and forgoing your own decisions for the sake of benefitting someone else, you should hold firm to your boundaries and do what's best for yourself, even if it creates feelings of guilt.

If you constantly give yourself away, it's likely that resentment will start to build inside you, and resentment rots relationships.

It's hard to get close to someone you resent.

It's hard to love someone you resent.

So if the choice is between feeling guilty about protecting myself or sacrificing myself for someone else, if I can tell that the sacrifice would lead to resentment, I'll choose guilt every time.

---

[48] Maté, G. (2003). *When the body says no: The cost of hidden stress*. Wiley.

Conclusion

Do you want to live a life you love?

It won't be easy, and it will take intentionality and hard work, but I promise it will be worth it.

"You do not rise to the level of your goals.
You fall to the level of your systems."
-James Clear

Life is full of rules, spoken and unspoken, explicit and implied.

We make them, break them, ignore them, and enforce them. And we all live by them.

Laid out inside this book is the set of rules that I choose to live by – a framework for how I make decisions. These rules bring me more peace and less stress; more of what I want and less of what I don't.

These rules have also been constructed over the course of many years, drawing on teachings from countless authors, speakers, pastors, friends, and family.

With these rules, I have peace of mind knowing that I'm choosing the life I want instead of others telling me what life to live.

As I stated earlier, we all have a certain way of living. Is it *your* way of living? Or is it someone else's?

I want you to have the courage to live the way you want to. I want you to live a life you love.

So if you've enjoyed some of the rules I live by and want to adopt them for your own – that's amazing.

If you found yourself saying, "That's great for him but not for me," I applaud that as well.

Whatever your opinion is about my rules, I hope you take this book as a starting point for creating or refining the set of rules you choose to live by.

Maybe you, too, can establish some rules around your work, your relationships, and your soul. Maybe you want to add some rules around your morning routine, your commute, or your parenting style.

I recommend identifying the most important parts of your life and creating rules and systems that will help you experience them in the way you want.

Don't let life happen to you. Decide what you want for your life.

The life you have is a direct result of the systems and rules you've put in place.

Your life is designed to get you exactly the results you're getting now.

Are they the results you want?

If not, what are you going to do to change them?

I suggest establishing some rules for your life and sticking to them.

Acknowledgements

"Anytime you see a turtle on top of a fence post, you know he had some help." -Alex Haley

---

This book was an incredible endeavor for me. In the middle of maintaining healthy relationships, completing class readings and assignments, and meeting deadlines, I was determined to finish this book.

Fortunately, I had a few things going for me:

> 1) Leading up to when I began writing, the frequency of how often I referenced these rules kept floating to the top of my mind, so it was easy to bring it all into focus.

> 2) This book is incredibly personal. I live by these rules on a daily basis, which makes it much easier to put into words than spending months doing research and crafting a compelling argument; this book is just my thoughts on paper.

> 3) I had an amazing group of people supporting me along the way!

First, I want to thank my beautiful and talented wife, Bree. She is the creative and organizational force behind this book, heading up most of the editing and all of the layout, design, and publishing. These words would still be in my head if not for you. I'm beyond blessed to have you as my teammate and partner, and marrying you has been my greatest choice, by far. I love you.

Next, thank you to my friend, Aaron Eldridge, for holding me accountable throughout the writing process, checking in on a weekly basis, and challenging me when I fell behind or when I needed to take a different direction.

I especially want to thank my parents, Duane and Christine Van Dyke. You set an example for me that shaped my life in every way. I can't fully describe how much your guidance has made me the man I am today.

My second editor, Barbara Clements – thank you for lending your expertise to help me clarify my ideas and strengthen the early manuscripts. As one of the first people to see these ideas in writing, thank you for being so kind and compassionate in helping me find my way.

My mentors, Mark Isder and Matt Douglas – thank you for spending countless hours with me discussing life, celebrating wins and sharing sorrows, and helping me grow in ways I didn't know were possible.

My best friends, Zach Gilreath and Ethan Heintz – you guys have sharpened me for over 20 years. We've laughed, we've cried, and we've truly shared life together. You've helped me become a better man, better husband, better friend, and better disciple.

Thank you to my early readers and feedback-givers, including Matt Douglas and Aaron Eldridge, as well as Dr. Dakota Witzel, Dr. Kevin Fullerton, Neil Downey, Casey Klocek, Miles Olofson, Gaby Axtman, Anders Barton, and Spencer Wirth. The book made sense in my head, but your valuable feedback helped me refine my ideas so they would make more sense for everyone else.

I couldn't have done any of this without the people on this list. Thank you all for being part of this journey.

Jason Van Dyke has spent over a decade supporting individuals through life transitions and personal challenges. As a counselor in training, he specializes in helping people build meaningful relationships and lives they are proud of. His approach centers on allowing lasting change to bloom from a deeper and more authentic understanding of ourselves.

Jason lives in South Dakota with his wife, where they enjoy relaxing at local coffee shops, volunteering in their church, and connecting with their community.

Instagram: @rightbraindev | X: @rightbraindev

Made in the USA
Monee, IL
26 July 2025

21960530R00069